M000309733

QUOTABLE SCRIBE

~ + ~

JAMES THOMAS ANGELIDIS

"every scribe who has been trained for the kingdom of heaven is like a householder who brings out of his treasure what is new and what is old."

-- Jesus Christ (Matthew 13:52)

QUOTABLE SCRIBE

JAMES THOMAS ANGELIDIS

jtangelidis.com

Cover Art
One Bookcase from JTA's Library
of 900 Books (Approx.)

AUTHOR BIO

James Thomas Angelidis has been awarded three university degrees and has authored and independently published several Christian books. These accomplishments helped him become a Professor of Christian Theology at Seton Hall University in South Orange, New Jersey. Discover James's works on his website at www.jtangelidis.com.

PREFACE

Artistic, intellectual, accessible and collectible -
Quotable Scribe is an ideal introduction to the
literature of James Thomas Angelidis. Over 100
original quotes from his works on topics such as…
immortality, eros, books, art, sport, nature, theology,
Salvation and Jesus Christ.

CONTENTS

~ 1 ~

New Cosmic Order

The promise of the Messianic Age came to fruition with our Lord. This coming age was already present in Christ who performed signs trumpeting His arrival as the sovereign ruler of the Jewish nation. By transforming water into wine, He made Himself known and thereby begins a new age, with a new cosmic order in which Christ our Lord is King and God.

-- JTA, *In the Name of Salvation, The Supreme Transformation*

~ 2 ~

Israel Personified

The Jewish nation sees itself as God's Chosen Servant. During moments of ecstasy and affliction it is obedient to God's will. It never questions God's plan and accepts its fate. On the Cross, Jesus represents the nobility and affliction of the Jewish nation. He becomes God's Chosen Servant. He is the perfect Jew and represents everything a Jew should be. Below are two passages from Isaiah that talk about God's Chosen Servant. In them, the Jewish nation sees itself and Christians see Jesus. … (Isaiah 42:1-4) … (Isaiah 52:13-53:12) … As the Messiah, Jesus is the embodiment of Israel. He is Israel personified. He is the culmination of Israel, its fulfillment and everything it was meant to be.

    -- JTA, *In the Name of Salvation, The Messiah Jesus*

~ 3 ~

Jesus Christ's Wine

Christ is the Jewish nation's salvation. He is the only fruitful vine. The Jewish nation failed to produce fruit [Isaiah 5:1-7], so Christ stepped in and took action [Psalm 80:8-19]. The wine that Christ produced is extraordinary and is the awaited celebratory wine of the triumphant Messianic Age [John 15:1-17] [Joel 3:18] [Amos 9:13-14].

-- JTA, *In the Name of Salvation, The Supreme Transformation*

~ 4 ~

Jesus was a Reader

Jesus was a reader.

-- JTA, *jtangelidis.com blog*

~ 5 ~

Abraham Lincoln

Lincoln was an avid reader. Lincoln grew up in the American frontier where skills with an axe and hunting were prized, not education. Most children who grew up like him found no value in books because their parents did not find them important, but Lincoln was an exception. Though tall and strong, he had dreams beyond the frontier and he believed that reading would make his dreams a reality. And, when most boys were idling away time, Lincoln was reading diligently. During the summer, he would read outside and at night, he would read under a lamp. He was curious, read with tenacity and reveled in the acquisition of knowledge… He was different than most boys and by the time he was nineteen, he had an idea that he would be a great man.

-- JTA, *Young Ezekiel, Storge*

~ 6 ~

Books Endure

… books are the most enduring art form. Homer wrote the *Iliad* and the *Odyssey* around 2800 years ago and they still live, stir the human spirit and speak to the soul. As readers today, we can benefit from the wisdom of the people who lived before us. Books make learning about the world, humanity and oneself possible and more complete. And, the best have the potential to pass the test of time, which is the most demanding and authoritative test I know.

-- JTA, *Young Ezekiel, Storge*

~ 7 ~

School Library

the school library... gave me access to thousands of books for free. I could reference dozens of books without leaving the building. It made it easy to build, expand and focus my knowledge and compare histories, ideas and philosophies. I could jump from the Chinese dynasties to communist Russia, from classical Greece to modern Germany. I could explore at my own pace; sometimes in an excited frenzy and sometimes in deep hard contemplation. I was hungry for knowledge and at times, I wanted to physically consume the books as if, with every swallow, the answers would come to me more quickly.

-- JTA, *Young Ezekiel, Eros*

~ 8 ~

Struggle in Books

in the school library … some of the books were worn because of their popularity; while, others were covered in dust. On the shelves, every book was a coffin with words inside, but once one was opened, it found air and was given new life. In each book, death and immortality fought every time a patron entered the library.

-- JTA, *Young Ezekiel, Eros*

~ 9 ~

Music

Music is the strongest medium that speaks to the soul. Books, at their best, teach us about the human condition, but music has the power to amplify or change our condition within an hour depending on what we need. There is always a song that we can connect with no matter what mood we are in. It might be because of the lyrics, the melodies or the rhythms that make us feel alive. It's more than sound because it is an expression of the human spirit. A talented musician is acutely in tune to what is inside of him and creates to share that with his audience. Sometimes, it is so personal that he may not want others hear his music, but if he does and it resonates with others, few things are as unifying. He is a kindred spirit that can hear what is inside of you and speaks for you. Few things can bring people together the way a good song does. Music is the most potent art form. Within seconds, a good song can reach the soul; however, it is the most fleeting art form. It changes with the times. It's like a flashing spark of light that excites, but disappears as quickly as it appeared.

-- JTA, *Young Ezekiel, Storge*

~ 10 ~

John Coltrane

From its birth, jazz has had soul in it. The artist's honesty and nakedness while performing his piece makes it impossible to not come from the soul. Coltrane, though, elevated jazz's spiritual possibilities and brought that soulful quality to the forefront. His album *A Love Supreme* ends with his track, "Psalm" - praising God's Supreme Love for us. The album is not a peaceful expression, rather an exuberant excitement of devotion to God. It's a piece of art that stands alone, that demands attention, that leaves an impression.

-- JTA, *Young Ezekiel, Storge*

~ 11 ~

Soul Rebel

It was an album of some of Bob Marley's early recordings with songs I never heard before. When I returned home and listened to the album, I noticed that the rhythms were uplifting and the lyrics were spiritual. Much of his music hit home. It was like medicine to my sick soul. I was hooked when I heard the song, "I'm Hurting Inside" because I, too, hurt inside. We were coming from the same place, so when Marley sang, "One Love! One Heart! Let's get together and feel all right," I knew things would get better. He preached love, peace, unity, freedom and Jah (God). In songs such as "Thank You Lord," he proclaimed how he loved to pray. Songs like "Exodus" are powerful and helped me make it through tough times. He was not a saint. He was notorious for smoking marijuana and having affairs with women; even so, most of his music is angelic. The youth are impressionable and Marley's indiscretions may seem cool, but my friends and I did not admire him for the marijuana and women; we thought he was cool because of his music.

-- JTA, *Young Ezekiel, Philia*

~ 12 ~

Bob Marley and God

I have listened to Bob Marley's music on a regular basis for the past 14 years. He and John Coltrane have perennially been my favorite musicians. A keyword to listen for in a Bob Marley song is "Jah," also known as "Yah," which is short for "Yahweh" (the proper name of God in the Hebrew Bible). Bob Marley was not just about marijuana and women. He loved and preached Jah (God) and that sets him apart from all other popular musicians and makes him special.

-- JTA, *jtangelidis.com blog*

~ 13 ~

Life is Both Art and Sport

Life is both art and sport and the more we put into it, the greater the masterpiece. We just have to care about life to make our lives worth living.

-- JTA, *Young Ezekiel, Eros*

~ 14 ~

Art

I thank God for art. God knows how hard life can be and I believe He gave us art - in its many forms - not to be a distraction, but to help us make it through. Plus, art enriches life.

  -- JTA, *jtangelidis.com blog*

~ 15 ~

Sport

Few things are as beneficial to youth as participating in sport. It teaches discipline, dedication and drive.

-- JTA, *jtangelidis.com blog*

~ 16 ~

Michael Jordan

One of my favorite people at work was Olivia - the lady at the greeting desk in the lobby. We had the same work schedule. She was a heavy lady, very sociable and well liked. She was also a big basketball fan, like me. One morning, I walked into the hospital's lobby and she saw me and asked,

"Ezekiel, honey, did you see Michael Jordan last night?"

"I certainly did. He scored 49 points," I answered.

"He's a pleasure to watch. I look forward to Chicago Bulls games," she said.

"Who would you rather see win, the Philadelphia 76ers or the Chicago Bulls with Michael Jordan?" I asked.

"Ezekiel, honey, you know I am a Philly native, but I have to admit: I sometimes catch myself cheering for Michael Jordan. I just hope he takes it easy on my Sixers," she replied.

"I understand," I said with a chuckle.

-- JTA, *Young Ezekiel, Eros*

~ 17 ~

Beach

No other place in Omorfi affected me as much as the beach I played on as a boy. As I got closer to it, I could smell and taste the salt water air, which tantalized my anticipation of my desired destination. I remember stepping on the sun beaten sand and it being hot. The vibrant sun was mightier than any cloud in the sky. The drifting clouds seemed to disappear in despair because they could not compete with the sun. I hurried through the grainy pebbled earth to the ocean's edge to relieve my feet's bottoms. The stark contrast of the hot sand to the cold water would tingle my feet, shoot up my legs, pass through my spine and flutter into my heart making me feel alive. The excitement of being at the beach was equally emotional and physical.

-- JTA, *Young Ezekiel, Philia*

~ 18 ~

Ocean

I remember being fixated on the rhythmic waves and moment by moment, they would rush on to the shore gently covering and refreshing my feet. The waves would console me - "Shhh… Shhh… Shhh" is what they would say - reassuring me that all is good. I stood there for a bit and watched the water approach me and then recede. Slowly, it would breathe in and just as it caught its breath, it would exhale with relentless consistency. Sometimes, the tide is high and sometimes, it is low, but I would never say that the ocean gets tired because it never stops. It never gives up. The ocean knows better than anyone that life is not a sprint. It is a marathon. It knows that tomorrow is another day. The ocean has been around longer than life itself and it marches on with confidence. I do not know what will happen tomorrow, but the ocean might. It is older, stronger and wiser than I am. I stood in front of the water and looked out to the ocean looking for answers and they came to me. My cares seemed to drift away with the wind. The ocean whispered to me reassuring me that all is not lost. It told me that there are things that I do not know, but that I should not lose faith. My heart murmured inside me, "meditation, meditation, meditation." I trust the ocean because it has never lied to me. Before I reached the ocean, my mind was in a fuss, but as I stood there gazing at and pondering into the triumphant ocean, it knew what to say to me to return my mind to peace. Day and night I see it in my mind's eye. As I approached it, it reminded me that it has answers.

-- JTA, *Young Ezekiel, Philia*

~ 19 ~

Stars

Nothing on earth is wiser than the ocean, but in all of Creation, nothing is wiser than the stars. They dwell in the heaven of heavens and shine bright reminding me of God's Eternity. I look up to them and like the ocean, they speak to me. The stars are kind, gentle and have never let me down. They do not run. They shine unapologetically. Even the ocean listens to the stars because the stars oversee it, too. I look up and the stars bring me to the edge of my thoughts encouraging me to find my own answers. The stars, tranquil and sublime, speak softly and humbly to me. Sometimes, I think I found the answers on my own, but when my troubles return, I know I must go to the stars who know me better than I know myself.

-- JTA, *Young Ezekiel, Philia*

~ 20 ~

Waking Up

When I was little, every day was special and every
Saturday morning was like a holiday. On Saturdays, I
would wake up early without any outside notice -
only from my exuberant spirit that could barely wait
to begin the day. Slowly, my eyes would open and a
smile would break through from within and surface
onto my face. I would take a deep breath and inhale
the sunlit air that filled my bedroom and yawn a great
yawn to fight drowsiness's gravity, which wanted to
keep me under the sheets. I would stretch my body
straight from the curl it kept itself in during the night,
feeling my blood flow through my veins, regenerating
my muscles. The light outdoor breeze would strike
the palm tree's leaves, which in turn would break the
wind. I could hear the confrontation of nature's
elements, which seemed to encourage me to get out of
bed. I could hear the birds chime into nature's
rhythmic commotion and sometimes a bird would
peep through the window and chirp hello. My spirit
and nature seemed to start the day together and begin
the first page of the day's chapter unified. I would
savor the surreal quality of my dreams and dance with

it until my mind's eye lit out the cloudiness of unreality and dusted off sleep's final phase.

-- JTA, *Young Ezekiel, Storge*

~ 21 ~

Butterfly Kisses

We would lovingly give each other butterfly kisses -
eyelash kisses on the cheek. It would tickle, but that
was how we greeted each other on Saturday
mornings.

-- JTA, *Young Ezekiel, Storge*

~ 22 ~

Young Ezekiel

What is love?
Can you describe it?
Do you love your parents, friends, romantic partner
and God in the same way?

In the English language, we use the word love in all
these relationships, but the ancient Greeks - the first
western philosophers - tried to capture, pinpoint and
distinguish the different forms of love with four
words: storge, philia, eros, agape.

In *Young Ezekiel: A Life of Loves*, Ezekiel will tell
you about his life and loves. Though his life is
unique, his relationships are like ours and, maybe,
through his story, you will learn about yourself and
the loves in your life.

-- JTA, *Young Ezekiel, Preface*

~ 23 ~

Love Vs Lust

God knows my heart wanted to love, but my mind was poisoned with lust. Love and lust are not the same. Love comes from the soul, while lust is all physical. Love is about both people in the relationship, while lust is just about oneself. If one is only concerned with what one can get, the relationship between the couple is doomed. Lust has no positive attributes - it only corrupts male and female. It is fantasy and deception that is contrary to love. Fleeting and ultimately unfulfilling, lust is one of the greatest lies. Because of my sexual liaisons with the girls, my confidence grew and I thought of myself as a real man, but I was far from being a real man, I was far from God.

-- JTA, *Young Ezekiel, Eros*

~ 24 ~

Know Thyself

Aunt Gerontissa knew what was inside of people because she was keenly aware of herself and to know oneself is to know what is inside others. As Socrates learned from the oracle of Delphi, "Know thyself." To know thyself is to know what dwells inside the individual and to know the human condition. She believed that we are all the same - we are all human beings all living on the same planet. We all experience love and pain and we can all relate to each other's joy and sorrow. She was sensitive to her own feelings and the feelings of others which gave her compassion. To know thyself is easier said than done. It could take a lifetime, but if one perseveres, one will notice treasures multiplying within.

-- JTA, *Young Ezekiel, Philia*

~ 25 ~

Street Smart and Wise

Aunt Gerontissa… was street smart. From her life experiences, she gathered information and saw patterns of when people prevailed and lost that helped her to make better decisions. She observed the piety of the priest, the erudition of the scholar, the lasciviousness of the whore and the greed of the miser. No one is perfect and she noticed when the priest was lazy and when the scholar was foolish and she observed redemption in the whore's honesty and the miser's frugality. She applied what she learned to her own life, which made her wise.

-- JTA, *Young Ezekiel, Philia*

~ 26 ~

Connections in the "Real World"

For a while, I felt lost. The direction I was heading towards was not leading to anything. I had few "connections" that could have led to a "job." Though I was not "working," I began to make connections in my mind of how I saw the world. I used the information I learned in school and early on in the "real world" little by little, I made connections regarding money and success and aspirations. Relationships appeared and I began to formulate in my mind an idea of the life I wanted to lead… as I tried to figure out what was real and not fake, true and not false.

-- JTA, *Writings, A Theological Memoir*

~ 27 ~

Time Well Spent

I studied and restudied 17 sacred texts as well as other religious literature from the 6 major world religions in 2 years. As a result, I produced my article "A Theological Memoir" - which is filled with portions of the scriptures - in my book *Writings* for the public.

A Theological Memoir

"A Theological Memoir" is the first of three articles in my book *Writings*. It is about my everyday-two-year journey through the six great world religions' sacred scriptures. It is reflection and is the first document I created that has been published. The work is significant and relevant.

-- JTA, Advertisements for *Writings, A Theological Memoir*

~ 28 ~

Spiritual Labor

As I accrued all this information about the great
world religions, connections between them became
apparent and the world became a smaller place. I was
growing spiritually and confidently. I believed that
the religions that I was learning were making me
wiser. As I was growing up, I desired physical
strength, but now, I sought mental and spiritual
strength. My priorities had changed and I devoted
myself to the teachings of God seeking the fruits of
my spiritual labor.

-- JTA, *Writings, A Theological Memoir*

~ 29 ~

Close to God

I spent day and night learning about God and His ways and I felt closer to Him than ever before. Reading those amazing books was like finding treasure. There were nights that I could barely sit still because I was so elated by the jewels of wisdom and theology revealed in those sacred texts.

-- JTA, *Writings, A Theological Memoir*

~ 30 ~

Becoming a Christian

when one discovers Jesus as the Christ, all other knowledge is unfulfilling. When one accepts Jesus as the Christ, the goal is no longer the acquisition of knowledge or anything else; rather, it is to be his loyal servant.

-- JTA, *Young Ezekiel, Eros*

~ 31 ~

Helping Children

I told her my favorite teacher, when I was young, made me believe I could be great one day. As an adult, her voice stayed with me and she made me believe in myself. When I doubted myself or failed, I thought of her. The greatest adults help children see their potential. It is like planting seeds and strengthening roots. It worked for me and is something I pass on to those younger than me.

-- JTA, *Young Ezekiel, Eros*

~ 32 ~

Teachers

Father believed in his profession, in cultivating the young minds of his students who will one day shape the world. He understood he may not make history, but he taught his students that one day they could.

-- JTA, *Young Ezekiel, Storge*

~ 33 ~

Philosopher King

I relished in my books and was most enchanted with philosophy. It was exhilarating to read 5th century BC Greek philosopher Plato's *The Republic* and I saw myself as a philosopher king.

-- JTA, *Young Ezekiel, Eros*

~ 34 ~

Dante's Allegory

The narrative of the *Divine Comedy* describes Dante's journey through the deepest depths of Hell, up Mount Purgatory and then to Heaven where God dwells. This narrative is an allegory for every individual in this world, for his journey and often times, his struggle to find peace in this world with the hope of Salvation.

-- JTA, *Writings, Dante's Divine Comedy*

~ 35 ~

Three Lights

Dante's three guides [during his journey through Hell, Purgatory and Heaven] ... represent the three lights in the world that help people see - with the brightest light at highest height that we can reach. The protagonist Dante sees what he sees because of the guides. They show him. Through them, he sees. These guides allegorically represent the light of Reason, the light of Faith and the light of Glory. They are the means to union with God. Dante is an artist at the highest level because through his art he is able to teach.

-- JTA, *Writings, Dante's Divine Comedy*

~ 36 ~

Heaven and Hell as Described by Dante

The saints dwell in God's unmitigated love. Furthest from the saints and God's love is Satan who resides at the bottom of Hell's pit. He is frozen to his waist in ice. Hell is the coldest place in the universe, so cold that the condemned - isolated from each other and alone - cannot move or speak. The exception is Satan who beats his bat-like wings keeping Hell and all the condemned forever frozen. Heaven is the opposite. It is at the highest of highests where space and time do not exist. It is a bright comforting euphoric community. God dwells in the Empyrean with the angels and saints who sit on the petals of a snow-white rose. God's everlasting love is everywhere and in everything. What is better than love? Nothing. It is free, yet the most valuable thing in the universe. This is the reason why Dante wrote the poem, so we would journey toward God's light, warmth and love. Satan's torture is not the darkness or cold. It is the madness and insanity that drowns him because he will never again see God. He will never again be comforted by Him or be a part of His love. There is no place worse than Hell because it is a place without God.

-- JTA, *Writings, Dante's Divine Comedy*

~ 37 ~

Saints

The saints in this world devote their lives to God because nothing else compares to Him. All else is superfluous in comparison to God, who alone is worthy of adoration and adulation. Every Christian in this world is called to become a saint. Dante's encounter with God is meant to be the goal for every Christian, but each Christian must seek it and journey toward it in order to experience it.

-- JTA, *Writings, Dante's Divine Comedy*

~ 38 ~

Serving God

Every day, I try to serve God. There are many ways to serve Him. We are each gifted with different strengths. The Christian saints are proof of this. No two saints are the same. Each is a person with his or her own identity, but each one serves God. I read and write and try to help those in need. Your path may be different. I tell you to take life seriously and get to know yourself. Find your passion and become all you can be. Take that passion and direct it toward God. Make God your first priority and everything else will work itself out. As long as God's love is in you and it remains in you, you will not go wrong.

-- JTA, *Writings, A Theological Memoir*

~ 39 ~

Holy Trinity in the Old Testament

Evidence of Holy Trinity theology (Almighty God as Father, Son and Holy Spirit) in the Old Testament clearly appears in Isaiah 9:6,

6 For to us a child is born,
   to us a son is given;
and the government will be upon his shoulder,
   and his name will be called
"Wonderful Counselor [Holy Spirit], Mighty God,
   Everlasting Father [Father], Prince of Peace [Son]."

The Holy Trinity is Jewish theology that Jesus of Nazareth elaborated on as [God the Son and the Christian Church crystalized in doctrine. It] is of principal importance. We are witnesses.

   -- JTA, *jtangelidis.com blog*

~ 40 ~

Jesus

I was inspired by my heroes and I would cry when I heard about their greatness. There was kinship between me and my heroes in the world - revolutionaries, athletes, artists, musicians - because I, too, wanted to be great and at times, I saw their greatness in me... All my heroes had a passion for life and each one touched my soul. But, no one meant more to me than my Lord Jesus the Christ who taught me about God and the true love between God and man and love between neighbors.

-- JTA, *Writings, A Theological Memoir*

~ 41 ~

Son's Reward

... (Matthew 10:40-42) ... But, I say to you that Jesus is not just a righteous man and he is more than a prophet; he is the Son of God and he who receives the Son of God because he is the Son of God shall receive the Son's reward. All who believe in Jesus and live according to his teachings will be given the right to enter Paradise because they acknowledge him as the Way, the Truth and the Life. He is the Door of the Sheepfold and all who enter through him will enter Paradise.

-- JTA, *Writings, A Theological Memoir*

~ 42 ~

Glory to Thee, Our God

There are many leaders - both good and bad - in the world, but Jesus is the only Christ and Son of God. He is the strongest man ever for no one else can be crucified as he was and retain his love for God the way he did with patience and grace. He is our Savior, who saves our souls from hell, death and eternal suffering. It is a sublime mystery that God chose to humble himself to become man - for Jesus truly was God. And, a still deeper tragic glory that he died, so we could have life. He entered this world to teach and show us the meaning of agape and since his advent, the world has never been the same. Glory to thee, our God, glory to thee.

-- JTA, *Young Ezekiel, Agape*

~ 43 ~

Humility Epitomized

My King is the Son of the Most High, yet he was stepped on like dirt. He suffered many things for me. The soldiers spat on him. How could they spit on my King? He lowered himself for me. Who am I? I am little and he is great. A devoted servant would lay down his life for his king, but my King laid down his life for his servants. What have we done to deserve such grace? How can we repay him? The only way I know how to repay him is to emulate him. We must be willing to sacrifice ourselves for him and the brethren. They treated him less than a human being when in reality he was God. It makes no sense, but if you listen to his words, you will see he did it out of agape. He was disgraced, but that is why I glorify him.

-- JTA, *Young Ezekiel, Agape*

~ 44 ~

Flood of Tears

I knew that Jesus was the Christ - God's Anointed One - when I discovered the Old Testament prophecy of God's Suffering Servant. It depicts Jesus's suffering and death and his mission and scope - even though it was written over 500 years before he arrived. It reads ... (Isaiah 52:13-53:12) ... When I first read this, my heart broke open and a flood of tears poured out. I could barely read it once, but when I did, I needed to read it again and again. Truly, Jesus is the Christ. He fulfills the Old Testament promise. He replaces Israel as the means of Salvation. He is God's Suffering Servant.

-- JTA, *Writings, A Theological Memoir*

~ 45 ~

Mothers

Raising a child is the toughest job in the world. To every child, mother is most important. Everyone says his or her mother is the best. Even in his song "Dear Mama," rapper Tupac Shakur praises his mother, a woman many would criticize. It's a deep and sensitive song from a self-proclaimed ghetto thug. Tupac Shakur and I grew up very differently, but I can relate to his song because I have the same love for my mother as he did for his mother. I do not know what it is about mothers. I am not a mother. Where do they get their love? Is it innate? Though often overlooked and taken for granted, no job is more serious and important.

-- JTA, *Young Ezekiel, Storge*

~ 46 ~

Children

No one chooses to be born.
A child enters the world
not knowing what is going on.
But, it is up to those who have come before the child
to make the world beautiful for him or her
and to save the child from the hell that exists...

   -- JTA, *Approaching the Kingdom, The Child's Soul*

~ 47 ~

Creating

Creating is one of humankind's most divine acts.
God created and we instinctively follow His example.
It sets us apart from animals
and makes us like Him.
Some people create families, businesses, buildings,
armies, art…
…We human beings are compelled and driven to
create,
like God.
It is the divine part of us manifest.
And, that which we create in life
defines us in the end.

  -- JTA, *Approaching the Kingdom*, *The Act of Creating*

~ 48 ~

Artistic Muse

...The power of artistic muse
is as euphoric as eros
and, like when in love,
the artist does not know where it is going to lead.
The process of creation
began with inspiration
aroused in me exaltation
with the goal of education
and edification.
It is unbridled imagination
stimulated by reflection
and is an exploration
for original work...

-- JTA, *Approaching the Kingdom, The Act of Creating*

~ 49 ~

Writing

Writing is sculpting, molding, painting, illustrating
and composing.
It is searching for and finding words,
structuring sentence and
fashioning paragraphs.
It is a discipline and craft.
Some people's dreams are bigger than those of others.
Constantine created an empire that lasted
for over 1000 years.
I put words, ideas and theology on paper
to lead people to God.
Some may say it was done in vain,
as the Preacher said,
"Vanity of vanities! All is vanity."
But, it was my natural inclination from many years
of reading and learning,
to share what saved me.

-- JTA, *Approaching the Kingdom, The Act of Creating*

~ 50 ~

Pen is Powerful

I believe there is truth in the proverb, "The pen is mightier than the sword." The damage done by the emperor's sword can be rectified by the writer's pen. Nothing can replace a life lost by the sword, but with the help of the pen, the story of that life can teach, inspire and unveil truth that can save many lives. When the emperor dies, so does his sword, as does his power and his influence on the world; yet, the writer's pen can leave a lasting impression unto the ages. The ideas behind the pen can change the world; something, the emperor tries to do with his sword, but inevitably fails. Certainly, if we dig deeper, we can discover additional meanings within the proverb's words, but it is clear that the pen is powerful. The pen can make a difference in people's lives and with the help of God, I hope to make a difference in people's lives with my pen. I hope to give life.

-- JTA, *About* (has appeared at the beginning of JTA's books)

~ 51 ~

Jewish Man of Color

To the shock of some, Jesus was not a white European. In truth, he was a Jewish man of color born in Palestine. And, revered by most, Mary was a Jewish teen virgin of color who gave birth to God.

-- JTA, *Young Ezekiel, Agape*

~ 52 ~

La Pieta

She said, "We also stopped in Rome in Vatican City in Saint Peter's Basilica where there is one of Michelangelo's *Pietas*, which is powerful. It depicts a youthful Mother Mary - majestic and regal - as she cradles her lifeless son. She is sorrowful and in disbelief and with her hand's gesture, she says, "Look at my son. They have killed him." Her gesture also says, "Here he is. He has done it - that which he was meant to do." And, with her demeanor, she glorifies him. I never studied art formally, so I may sound naive, but Michelangelo's work spoke to me."

-- JTA, *Young Ezekiel, Eros*

~ 53 ~

Mahatma Gandhi

I wanted to be like these men - men like Mohandas Gandhi, the Mahatma, the Great Soul. He carried the Indian nation to freedom from the British Empire - one of the most powerful empires in recent history - without a sword. His wisdom paralleled that of King Solomon. It was said that during the peak of Hindu and Muslim strife in India, a Hindu anarchist confessed to Gandhi that he killed a Muslim child by smashing the child's head against a wall because the Muslims killed his son. Gandhi told the man that he knew a way out of Hell. He told the man, a Hindu, to find a Muslim boy, his enemy's son, whose parents had been killed in the strife and to raise and nurture the boy as his own, only to be sure that he, a Hindu, raise the boy to be a Muslim, the faith of this enemy. The brilliant Albert Einstein was quoted saying, "Generations to come will scarce believe that such a one as this ever in flesh and blood walked upon this Earth."

-- JTA, *Writings, A Theological Memoir*

~ 54 ~

The Supreme Transformation - Water into Wine

In the following treatise, I examine Christ's first miracle - transforming water into wine, which took place at a wedding in Cana in Galilee. This sign foreshadowed and illustrated his transformation of the natural rhythm of the cosmos. Ancient Chinese sages used the term Tao to refer to the natural rhythm of the cosmos and they observed that it behaved like water. The Tao's lofty esoteric principles were followed by few. But, there was tribulation in the world and Christ came into the world to save all people, not just the few. He transformed the Tao into what resembles wine to save lowly humankind from its sins. I believe if we can better understand the Tao, we will be able to better see the magnitude, magnificence and majesty of Christ. In writing this treatise, I hope to help my fellow Christians better understand our Lord through knowledge of the Tao and to help non-Christians, through the Spirit of Truth, begin to believe that Christ is the Son of the Most High God.

-- JTA, *In the Name of Salvation, The Supreme Transformation - Water into Wine* (back cover)

~ 55 ~

Agape into Eternity

The following treatise is meant to be a painting in words of the means to union with God. This way people can see the big picture, so there is no longer fear - only hope, comfort and peace - about eternity. The 3000 year old thriving Hindu theology of Brahman, Atman and Moksha is the image and Jesus is the way. I have not focused on Jesus's miracles or resurrection to illustrate his unique position as God's only begotten Son who makes eternal life possible. I have focused on his agape, which if embraced and emulated, will unite one with God who is Agape. Implicit in the theology is the Holy Spirit who, too, is Agape.

-- JTA, *In the Name of Salvation, Agape into Eternity* (back cover)

~ 56 ~

The Messiah Jesus

The title Messiah comes from the Hebrew word "mashiach," which means "anointed one." In Jewish tradition, it was used to refer to priests and kings who were anointed with holy oil to consecrate their positions and signify God's blessing. However, in the Jewish theology about the end of days, it has greater significance because it refers to the Messiah who will usher in God's Kingdom. The Greek term for the title Messiah is Christ. Jesus's followers identify Jesus as the Christ. They are known as Christians. In the following treatise, I display Old Testament passages about the Messiah and God's Kingdom of Heaven and how Jesus makes the prophecies reality. My goal is to strengthen my fellow Christians' faith and show Jews that Jesus is the One.

-- JTA, *In the Name of Salvation, The Messiah Jesus* (back cover)

~ 57 ~

Our Priest-King

Jesus is better than a political king who can gain territory or peace for his subjects in this world. He is our King and Priest who can save us from death and give us eternal life. Most did not understand this at first. Not even Jesus's disciples were fully aware of his eternal power. Not until Jesus rose from the dead and appeared to his disciples, did they fully understand his power. Truly, his kingship is not of this world. Jesus's reign is in the Kingdom of God and not in a kingdom of man.

-- JTA, *In the Name of Salvation, Agape into Eternity*

~ 58 ~

Palm Sunday

Palm Sunday is one of the most beautiful and moving days in the year for Christians. It commemorates Jesus's triumphal entry into Jerusalem trumpeting his arrival as our King, Savior and God. He enters the city sitting on a donkey announcing that he is the King that Jerusalem had been waiting for … (Zechariah 9:9) … The crowd that greeted Jesus glorified him shouting, "Hosanna! Blessed is he who comes in the name of the Lord! Blessed is the kingdom of our father David that is coming! Hosanna in the highest!" (Mark 11:9b). They spread palm tree branches on the ground and hailed him as their king.

  -- JTA, *Young Ezekiel, Agape*

~ 59 ~

Man of Sorrows

For Christians, Palm Sunday is a day to celebrate, but the days following Palm Sunday are sad because we know that our King will soon be killed.

-- JTA, *Young Ezekiel, Agape*

~ 60 ~

Authenticity of the Crucified Christ

...the details of Jesus's final hours and death are well documented. It is the most well documented period described in all four Gospels and one of the most well preserved events in human history. The death of the Christ can be difficult to fathom, but it is authentic. It does not agree with conventional human wisdom and can be difficult to make sense of, but it was instituted because of God's Providence and Wisdom. It is not an event that we may like or want to accept or be proud of unless we are seekers of truth. His role was prophesied in the Old Testament and he fulfilled it. Those who have examined the Jewish Scriptures know it and so do those who have seen his workings in the world. The Cross is fundamental.

-- JTA, *Young Ezekiel, Agape*

~ 61 ~

Savior

Pain and struggle add depth to the soul. Recovery is strength. Jesus makes recovery possible. He is Salvation.

-- JTA, *Young Ezekiel, Agape*

~ 62 ~

Christ is Risen

From one candle to the next, the once dark church
was filled with light and light overcame darkness, just
as Jesus has overcome death. For we Christians,
Jesus's death is the saddest day of the year, but his
resurrection is the most joyous.

-- JTA, *Young Ezekiel, Agape*

~ 63 ~

Blood

2nd century Church theologian Tertullian famously said that "the blood of the martyrs is the seed of the Church." The martyrs' bloody deaths and their strength to not deny their love for Christ propagated the faith. I can envision onlookers puzzled by a Christian martyr's death ask one another, "Who are these people who face death without fear and what do they believe in?" The answer that traveled the land was that they are Christians and they believe in Jesus the Christ.

-- JTA, *Young Ezekiel, Philia*

~ 64 ~

Footprints in the Sand

I believe God never leaves us, even when we think He has. This sentiment is illustrated in mother's favorite poem, *Footprints in the Sand*. In it, a man has a dream about his life with God of which is represented by two sets of footprints on a beach. He notices that during his most difficult times, there is only one set and so questions God's presence. The poem ends with God comforting and reassuring the man that when he saw only one set of footprints on the beach, it was not that God was not by his side, but rather that God was carrying him.

   -- JTA, *Young Ezekiel, Storge*

~ 65 ~

Saint Augustine and *The City of God*

The Bible is the book that has had the greatest influence on my life. Saint Augustine's *The City of God* is number two.

-- JTA, (social media)

With the City begins the Kingdom.

-- JTA, *Approaching the Kingdom, O, Saint Augustine*

~ 66 ~

My Sword

Truth is my sword.

-- JTA, *jtangelidis.com blog*

~ 67 ~

Four Loves

Though storge, philia and eros are noble, agape is divine.

-- JTA, *In the Name of Salvation, Agape into Eternity*

~ 68 ~

God's Love

…God's selfless self-sacrificial death
is agape love.
No one loves us more than God…

-- JTA, *Approaching the Kingdom, God's Supreme Love*

~ 69 ~

Devil

That which comes between you and agape is the devil.

-- JTA, *jtangelidis.com blog* (clarified)

~ 70 ~

Agape

Agape is everlasting because it comes from God. The other forms of love promise to be everlasting and when they are at their peaks, it is easy to believe them, but they do not follow through. My family's storge, my friends' philia and my girlfriends' eros deeply affected me and bettered my life, but the feelings I shared with them were confined by time and space and eventually faded. The power of agape endures. Even when it feels weak because God seems distant, I know it is there because I know God will never leave me. It is faith, but it is not blind faith. I trust Scripture, the Church and the testimonies of the saints who encourage me to stay strong and be patient because God is near. My storge for my family, my philia for my friends and my eros for the girls in my life have faded in time, but my agape for them has not. My agape for them remains in me. It is my moments of agape with them that make me smile during the day and help me sleep soundly at night. The agape I share with them is everlasting because its source is God. God gives us His agape, which we must reciprocate and also share with our neighbor. Even when we behave unlovable, agape remains.

Differences and disagreements may tarnish storge, philia and eros, but they will not tarnish agape. Agape is so pure that it does not get dirty.

-- JTA, *In the Name of Salvation, Agape into Eternity*

~ 71 ~

Thanking God

How does a man thank God…

-- JTA, *jtangelidis.com blog*

~ 72 ~

And the Lamb Spoke

Inspired by the children I worked with, *And the Lamb Spoke: Lessons from the Gospels* is about a boy named Basil who is sent to a children's home. After an incident with another child, Basil runs into the forest to get away from his troubles. Then, a Lamb appears. Basil has questions about life and the Lamb answers Basil's questions with Jesus's teachings found in the Gospels. The book has 15 lessons about topics such as love, giving and forgiveness. Each lesson is complemented with a living forest narrative that is sure to keep children engaged while teaching them. For ages 7 to 9, but adults can enjoy and learn from it, too!

    -- JTA, *And the Lamb Spoke* (back cover)

~ 73 ~

Lamb Spoke About God

Basil asked, "Tell me about God."

The Lamb answered, "Yes, my dear child...

... God is the Creator who created us and all things. For those who choose to listen to God, He becomes their Heavenly Father and they become His children and the angels rejoice. Great rewards in God's Kingdom of Heaven await those who listen.

At that moment in the forest, the sun grew bigger, twice as big as it was just a moment ago. The sunbeams grew brighter, twice as bright as they were just a moment ago. It was as if the sun heard the Lamb's words and liked what it heard and got closer to hear more of what the Lamb had to say.

-- JTA, *And the Lamb Spoke, God*

~ 74 ~

Living Forest Narrative

At that moment in the forest, a busy bubbly bumble bee buzzed by the blooming bud. It liked what it saw and nestled itself into the flower. Grateful, it hummed with happiness.

-- JTA, *And the Lamb Spoke, Forgiveness*

~ 75 ~

Good Shepherd

"Do you know who is the Good Shepherd, my young friend?" he asked.

"Of course, sir. It's Jesus," I answered.

"Do you know why he is called the Good Shepherd?" he asked.

"Not exactly, sir," I answered.

"It's because he laid down his life for us, his flock," he explained.

-- JTA, *Young Ezekiel, Agape*

~ 76 ~

God and Doubters

My parents did not follow an organized religion, but they believed in the Almighty God of the three great monotheistic world religions - Judaism, Christianity and Islam. They believed He is a Supreme Presence who plays a role in people's lives and that He is Powerful. Most people in the world believe in God and some do not and my parents felt bad for those who do not. Some people deny the existence of God through science. The reasoning mind and the senses are the foundation of science; however, my parents knew that the reasoning mind and the senses are not trustworthy. My parents recognized that science has achieved great things and that it has taught us much from the microscopic to the cosmic. And, they believed in the noble honesty of the scientific method and it's longing for truth to the point of confession of its limitations never knowing if its findings are completely correct. Conclusions are constantly being reassessed by means of new tests and discoveries. Science has not given us all the answers. And, it may never. With science, there is no end in sight. There will always be new realms to explore and more questions to ask. Science desires to see the whole iceberg even though, more often than not, it is only a witness of the iceberg's tip. Plato understood this and allegorized the weakness of perception in his allegory of the cave where people saw truth in shadows and not what was the source of the shadows. I believe that, eventually, science will find that everything began with God. And, I believe science will eventually realize that God will be the end of scientific discovery. Pope Benedict XVI professed that science is "unable to grasp the global nature of reality" (December 22, 2005). My parents believed that God is reality. They believed that God is beyond our comprehension and that He is mysterious, but that He does exist.

-- JTA, *Young Ezekiel, Storge*

~ 77 ~

Life's Goal

There is a triumph of truth's consistency among the great world religions that there is something with us that is greater than the universe, yet intimately connected to oneself. As a Christian, I believe this is God and that He is our Father, but the other great world religions are not wrong when they describe His Power. All the great world religions aim to unite us with God. Union with God is the reason for living and the final goal. However, it is only possible through Jesus the Christ who is the Way to God the Father.

-- JTA, *Writings, A Theological Memoir*

~ 78 ~

Union with God

Agape [love] is crucial for union with God. There are many ways to get close to God, but only agape can unite us with God. God is the source of agape and God's Son Jesus brings God's agape to earth. Jesus is agape Incarnate and perfectly revealed agape to the world through his life, suffering and death. To become one with God, we must become one with the Son. Becoming one with the Son is the only way to become one with God because the Son fills us with agape and only those who are filled with agape can become one with God who is Agape.

-- JTA, *In the Name of Salvation, Agape into Eternity*

~ 79 ~

Immortality

To become one with the immortal is to become immortal… It is like when a drop of water enters and becomes one with water… the Son [Jesus] fills us with agape [love] and only those who are filled with agape can become one with God who is Agape.

-- JTA, *In the Name of Salvation, Agape into Eternity*

~ 80 ~

We Can Make God Happy

God needs nothing. He has everything. But, there is one thing He desires: our agape. He has given us free will and we can choose Him or not and when a person chooses God, nothing brings God greater happiness. How sweet it is to know that we can make God happy! All was not for nothing. The Divine Plan has come to fruition. The made has returned to his Maker. God desires for us to have agape for Him in return because He knows the agape shared between He and us will bring us joy, which we know to be true from the testimonies of the saints.

-- JTA, *In the Name of Salvation, Agape into Eternity*

~ 81 ~

Old Testament Imagery

Jesus applied Old Testament imagery to his teachings and also used it to illustrate his role as the Messiah. In the Old Testament, Israel is described as God's Vine ... (Psalm 80:8-19) ... Jesus identifies himself as the above son of man who sits at the right hand of God. He calls himself the True Vine with his faithful as the branches that bear fruit and that God is the Vinedresser ... (John 15:1-17) ... Similarly, Jesus was aware of the Old Testament imagery of God as Shepherd who tends to His people, His flock ... (Ezekiel 34:1-31) ... As Jesus does with the Old Testament vine imagery, he uses the shepherd imagery to describe himself. He takes the shepherd imagery a step further and declares that he is the Good Shepherd who lays down his life for God's flock ... (John 10:1-18)

-- JTA, *In the Name of Salvation, The Messiah Jesus*

~ 82 ~

Divine Grace

… This alone is sublime
that Great God would choose to make Himself little -
an event we celebrate on Christmas.
But, then, in still deeper sublimity,
the Creator, who created us and all things,
decides, in His Most High Wisdom,
to sacrifice Himself for His creation.
… God's selfless self-sacrificial death
is agape love.
No one loves us more than God.
… How do we repay God
for this Divine act of Grace
that we do not merit
and are unworthy of?
How can we thank Him?
It is impossible.
But we must try.

-- JTA, *Approaching the Kingdom, God's Supreme Love*

~ 83 ~

Defining Success

There are two philosophies about success in life: work for money or do what you love. Some people are blessed and they make money by doing what they love, but for most, it is a fork in the road. The world tells us, "Make money" and I want to tell the world, "I have dreams." In our world, money is a necessity - it is how we share resources - but money should not be the goal. There will never be enough money. If a person can find a passion, he must not let it go to make money - the risk of losing his passion is too great.

-- JTA, *Young Ezekiel, Eros*

~ 84 ~

Inspiration

He believed inspiration is divine and transformative. It prompts people to act and if it remains, extraordinary things will happen. It is like supernatural motivation. It is a thought that ignites a flame in a person that has the potential to set a group and nation to rise and make change happen.

-- JTA, *Young Ezekiel, Storge*

~ 85 ~

Reading is Important

Reading is important. Books are important. You don't need degrees. You just need the hunger for knowledge and answers.

-- JTA, *jtangelidis.com blog*

~ 86 ~

Philosophy and Theology

Without the help of theology, philosophy does not understand the degradation of sin. Philosophy recognizes the distinction between virtues and vices and can even persuade one to live a virtuous life. It has that potential - but it is unconvinced. Theology is convinced that a virtuous life is the only way to live because it brings one closer to God. Philosophy does not know God. If it did, it would be theology. Philosophy can be purified through theology and will reach its full potential by means of theology, but philosophy without theology lacks God's blessings. Until philosophy embraces theology, it remains in Limbo.

-- JTA, *Writings, Dante's Divine Comedy*

~ 87 ~

First Date

We walked together down the road to the coffee shop. It was spring and there was a gentle breeze in the air. The sun was setting turning the sky into pale purple and pink. Feathery clouds caressed the sky, which was melting into the horizon. Beside the sidewalks, shrubs bloomed flowers and above, trees housed singing sparrows. It was a quiet neighborhood where bakers baked bread and window shopping was a pastime. People nodded hello and couples held hands. I was walking taller than usual with Julie by my side.

-- JTA, *Young Ezekiel, Eros*

~ 88 ~

Endearing Intimacies

We sat on the floor listening to music and telling stories. She hummed as she thought and such endearing intimacies made me feel like we had known each other forever. They are intimacies that not everyone gets a glimpse of or could appreciate, little things, like a gesture or look, that make eros special.

-- JTA, *Young Ezekiel, Eros*

~ 89 ~

First Kiss

We sat shoulder to shoulder. During a moment of silence between us, I slid my hand down her arm, extended my fingers and grasped her hand and she grasped mine.

> If I profane with my unworthiest hand
> This holy shrine, the gentle sin is this:
> My lips, two blushing pilgrims, ready stand
> To smooth that rough touch with a tender kiss
> (Shakespeare, *Romeo and Juliet*, 1.5.91).

She turned her head toward me and I leaned in. Then, we kissed. Paused. And, then, we kissed, again. From that moment, I was hers and she was mine.

-- JTA, *Young Ezekiel, Eros*

~ 90 ~

Classical Antiquity's Love Story

There is also a story of Eros [aka Cupid] who, as a young deity, falls in love with Psyche who falls in love with him. Love falls in love and is loved … It is one of the most famous love stories in classical antiquity … In Greek, "eros" means love and "psyche" means soul. When I learned this, the story of Eros and Psyche became more interesting and I wanted to see if I could learn anything about the relationship between love and the soul.

-- JTA, *Young Ezekiel, Eros*

~ 91 ~

University

During my first semester at the university, I noticed a change in myself. I was growing up. My clothes were more adult and I was standing taller. I developed a stride. It was the brash swagger of a college kid who was discovering his potential, but who had not yet been tested by the world. It was a wonderful time and everything was new. It was unknown territory for me and I was ready to explore.

-- JTA, *Young Ezekiel, Eros*

~ 92 ~

High Art

High Art
Reveals Truths
Enjoy...
Young Ezekiel:
A Life of Loves

    -- JTA, Advertisement for *Young Ezekiel* (social media)

~ 93 ~

Gospel Music's Depth and Power

Music was important in our house and was not neglected on Sundays. Black American Gospel music helped us get closer to God because of the musicians' devotion to God's Son Jesus the Christ and the music's message of the Good News of God's Kingdom of Heaven. Gospel music's depth and power cannot be denied. Those singers and musicians were not merely entertainers, but brothers and sisters who we related to in heavenly ecstasy and worldly pain. Mahalia Jackson, Aretha Franklin and the Five Blind Boys of Mississippi [also the Salem Travelers and the Staple Singers] kept us centered in this turbulent world and helped us get by during rough days.

-- JTA, *Young Ezekiel, Storge*

~ 94 ~

Confronting the Cross

At the time of death, we will each have to confront the Cross. And how we react will be a testimony to our eternal fates. The Cross represents Jesus's crucifixion and agape love for us. He is Salvation and if we can weep - like the saints - for the Good Shepherd King - with an agape love lived life - we, too, will be saved and enter His Kingdom and Paradise.

-- JTA, *jtangelidis.com, "The Good Shepherd King" Explained*

~ 95 ~

God's Mother

… God had a mother
and we call her the Theotokos.
She gave birth to Him,
raised, nurtured and loved Him.
She lives in all women
in this living world
because all women are compelled
to nurture and raise our children
to be living Christs.
Regardless of race, nationality or creed,
all women want to raise men -
strong and real men.
And, there was only one true and perfect man -
Jesus, who is
"Wonderful Counselor, Mighty God,
Everlasting Father, Prince of Peace" (Isaiah 9:6)
born of Mary, who is
Theotokos.
No other man comes close …

-- JTA, *Approaching the Kingdom, God's Mother - The Theotokos*

~ 96 ~

Jesus, An Erudite Jew

Jewish sage and scholar Hillel the Elder was born about 100 years before Jesus. He is quoted saying, "That which is hateful to you, do not do to your neighbor. That is the whole Torah; the rest is commentary. Go and study it." As an erudite Jew, Jesus knew of Hillel and his teachings. However, Jesus revolutionized Hillel's worldly proverb and made it divine by replacing hate with love. Jesus says, "So whatever you wish that men would do to you, do so to them; for this is the law and the prophets" (Matthew 7:12). Elsewhere, Jesus says, "You shall love your neighbor as yourself" (Matthew 22:39).

-- JTA, *In the Name of Salvation, The Messiah Jesus*

~ 97 ~

Sin

Sin is anything that
distances a person from God
or comes between a person and God.

-- JTA, *jtangelidis.com blog*

~ 98 ~

Truth

Truth is eternal
because
God is Truth

-- JTA, Advertisements for Books (social media)

~ 99 ~

My Work

It's about the message, not the money.

I believe my work can help serve God and the world in the Economy of Salvation.

I wrote my books out of agape for God and neighbor.

I wrote my books to share what saved me.

My books are meant to be a beginning, not an end.

My books are about survival and eternal life.

-- JTA, Advertisements for Books (social media)

~ 100 ~

Great Sower

God - the Great Sower - planted seeds across the world, seeds that took root and grew in the world's religions. Truths can be found in them all; however, what is said about the Jews is true - they were the Chosen People, they were God's Vineyard (Isaiah 5:1-7). For from them grew the True Vine - God's Son Jesus the Christ (Psalm 80:8-19) (John 15:1-17). I am just trying to be one of our Lord's branches and bear fruit for him because I love him so much. I believe my work can help serve God and the world in the economy of Salvation.

-- JTA, *jtangelidis.com, Church: In the Spirit of Truth*

~ 101 ~

Similarities in the World Religions

When I decided to examine the great world religions, I had an innate belief that they have similarities because we are all human beings all living on the same planet. Compassion, wellbeing and eternal wisdom are cornerstones of each of the great world religions. As Plato recognized, we all inherently seek the Good.

-- JTA, *Writings, A Theological Memoir*

~ 102 ~

Difference Among the World Religions

I learned that the great world religions can be classified into two types: those that come from human inquiry and those that are God attributed...
...the great difference between the religions that come from human inquiry and the religions that are God attributed is belief in the One Almighty God. The religions of human inquiry (Hinduism, Taoism and Buddhism) do not teach that there is One Almighty God; while, the religions that are God attributed (Judaism, Christianity and Islam) do teach that there is One Almighty God.

-- JTA, *Writings, A Theological Memoir*

~ 103 ~

Reason I Write

If there is any one James Thomas Angelidis book to buy for yourself, this is it. In *Approaching the Kingdom: An Anthology*, the reader will find all my works in one place. This 512 page volume is the result of a 15 year journey. This process began after college when I was 22 with my search for truth in the so called "real world." And, it includes my more recent letters and drawings. It is a comprehensive representation of my written efforts to save souls.

-- JTA, *Approaching the Kingdom, Preface*

~ 104 ~

My Plan

With this anthology, I have tried to make my books and other works as accessible as possible. It illustrates my vision and presents the way and order my books are meant to be read. My books are in target audience age order - the way I foresee my youngest fans growing up with my work. My plan has always been to raise generations of children, so they can ultimately become adults who are one with God, to save their souls, so they can attain eternal life. And, once they are saved, they can then also save others. This is my way of training young warriors for God.

-- JTA, *Approaching the Kingdom, Preface*

~ 105 ~

Anthology

In this anthology - *Approaching the Kingdom* - I have laid out the most important things that have helped me reach Salvation and this is my method of helping others attain Salvation. So, enjoy and may God bless you as he did with me when I created these works.

-- JTA, *Approaching the Kingdom, Preface*

~ ~ ~

Prophecy from the Book of Daniel

"Many shall run to and fro,
and knowledge shall increase."

-- A prophesying angel, probably Gabriel
(Daniel 12:4b)

~ ~ ~

Made in the USA
Columbia, SC
11 May 2021

37178825R00072